This Book Belongs To:

....

I am .... years old.

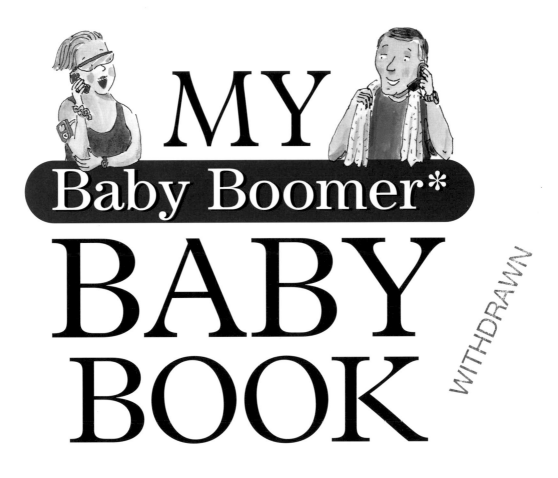

MY
Baby Boomer*
BABY BOOK

WITHDRAWN

* Ages 42 and Up

Mary-Lou Weisman

ILLUSTRATED BY PAUL MEISEL

Workman Publishing • New York

LIBRARY OF CONGRESS CATALOGING-IN-PUBLICATION DATA
IS AVAILABLE UPON REQUEST.

ISBN-13: 978-0-7611-4384-0
ISBN-10: 0-7611-4384-X

WORKMAN BOOKS ARE AVAILABLE AT A SPECIAL DISCOUNT WHEN PURCHASED
IN BULK FOR SPECIAL PREMIUMS AND SALES PROMOTIONS AS WELL AS FOR
FUND-RAISING OR EDUCATIONAL USE. SPECIAL EDITIONS OR BOOK EXCERPTS CAN
ALSO BE CREATED TO SPECIFICATION. FOR DETAILS, CONTACT THE SPECIAL
SALES DIRECTOR AT THE ADDRESS BELOW.

WORKMAN PUBLISHING COMPANY, INC.
225 VARICK STREET
NEW YORK, NY 10014-4381

MANUFACTURED IN CHINA

FIRST PRINTING OCTOBER 2006
10 9 8 7 6 5 4 3 2 1

ACKNOWLEDGMENTS

I'd like to take this opportunity to acknowledge all the middle-aged amnesiacs who have contributed to making this book an overnight bestseller. First I want to thank my editor, Ruth . . . Ruth . . . Darn! It's right on the tip of my tongue! . . . Oh, and I especially appreciate the expertise of gastroenterologist Dr. David . . . Ummm, David . . . And, of course, the host of friends too unforgettable to mention, not the least of whom is my patient, supportive husband . . . what's his name? . . .

CONTENTS

INTRODUCTION

In 1995, when the first 3.2 million Baby Boomers turned 50, reached for their reading glasses, their water bottles, and their cell phones, *My [Middle-Aged] Baby Book* was there to celebrate and chronicle this crucial developmental stage. The Internet barely existed. Googling was something babies did. A blackberry was edible, and, if you had a rotary phone, you could stay on the line and talk to a human.

Every aspect of the culture has changed radically. Eleven years ago, people weren't "folks," and Viagra wasn't in the vocabulary, never mind in the medicine cabinet. Now, it's "Good-bye" evolution, Venus and Mars, jogging, video cameras, privacy, CDs, anchor people, answering machines, Blockbuster, dating services, catalog buying, and frequent-flyer points.

And it's "Hello" cloning, domestic divas, performance-enhancing drugs, preemptive wars, spirituality, Netflix, QVC, e-dating, 24/7, 9/11, ringtones,

DVDs, rap, breast augmentation, tattoos, and teardowns.

And my how they've grown! In the past 11 years, some 35 million Baby Boomers (including the 4 million who will turn 50 this year) have been added to the ranks of Middle Age. They deserve to have—actually, they insist upon having—their own new, totally updated, expanded, unexpurgated, reborn Baby Boomer baby book, and they want it now. Where else can they celebrate the signal events of their middle years: their first colonoscopy, their first conservative opinion, chin hair, and liver spot? Where else can they record vital personal information: their body mass index, resting pulse, and reflexologist's cell phone number? What other book will tell them how to stay middle-aged forever?

While time marches on at warp speed, boomers have found a way to freeze-frame it, thanks to cosmetic surgery, nutritional supplements, and counting backward by tens. Fifty is the new 40; 60 the new 50; and, as soon as they get there, 70 will be the new 60. At this rate, or at least until generations yet unborn rise up and rcbcl against thcm for depleting the nation's financial resources by defying death, figure on a revision of *My [Baby Boomer] Baby Book* every decade.

My Vital Statistics

(PHOTO HERE)

Here I Am

I'm a girl .... boy .... *(check one)*

Name: ....
(FIRST)   (MIDDLE)   (FAMILY NAME)

Married name(s): ....

Address: ....

I live in a red state .... blue state ....

I am intelligently designed .... I am evolved ....

I am .... years old/not telling ....

Weight: .... Length: ....

Circumference of head: ....

Circumference of abdomen: ....

Inseam/Bra size: ....

Organ donor card: ....

Social Security number: ....

Driver's license: ....

PIN: ....

Credit cards: Visa .... Mastercard .... American Express ....

EXPIRATION DATES: ....

Phones: landline .... cell ....

      office .... car ....

  I am listed on the Do Not Call Registry: yes .... no ....

Fax: ....

Voicemail remote code: ....

E-mail: ....

Cholesterol count: ....

  Bad HDLs .... Good HDLs ....

Locker combination: ....

          (RIGHT)   (LEFT)   (RIGHT)

Blood pressure: ....

Body mass index (BMI): ....

Resting pulse: ....

DNA: ....

Memorable Firsts

My first tooth lost: ....

My first colonoscopy: ....

My first reading glasses: ....

My first gray hair: ....

My first gray pubic hair: ....

My first second mortgage: ....

My first isolated hiccup: ....

My first conservative opinion: ....

My first involuntary release of urine while sneezing: ....

My first cosmetic surgery: ....

My first: ....

My first: ....

My Bottle

Formula	Response
❑ BALVENIE SCOTCH Neat or one rock	Mellow
❑ CABERNET	Sleepy
❑ DIRTY MARTINI Vodka, olive juice, olive	Headachy
❑ PINOT GRIGIO	Chatty
❑ COSMOPOLITAN Vodka, Cointreau, cranberry juice, lime	Very chatty
❑ AMSTEL LIGHT	Burpy
❑ _____ _____ (OTHER)	

EAU CLAIRE DISTRICT LIBRARY

13

AM I A GIRL OR A BOY?

That depends. Do you spend most of your time in front of the toilet, running water, or naked on the lawn, rolling in snow?

Usually at about the age of 50, both men and women go through profound physical changes: women are no longer able to bear children and men are no longer able to pee. This is not bad. This is natural.

As is too often the case with matters involving sexuality, ignorance and fear are the worst enemies. Just a very few years ago, women wouldn't even talk among themselves behind closed doors about menopause. No one dared speak its name. They referred to it darkly as "the change." No one wanted to be associated with the stereotypical sexless, moody hag in a house dress who went about flinging open windows, hurling epithets, and sprouting chin hairs. But as soon as the first change-of-life revolutionary stepped out of the closet wearing a white silk blouse, hoop earrings, Manolo Blahniks, and a face-lift and spoke the words "Is it hot in here or is it me?" the dread taboo was broken. Menopause began to catch on. The hot flash acquired instant cachet. Watching one come and go became an event to rival a new episode of *The Sopranos* or the aurora borealis.

Hot was cool. Vaginal dryness was on *Oprah*. The public, once in love with celebrities who kept having each other's babies out of wedlock, now turned its fickle attention to celebrities who hot flashed in public. Reality TV quickly cashed in on the change with *Boiling Point,* a high-concept survival show in which scantily clad menopausal women, locked in a sauna, compete to find the key. It's only a matter of time before Shirley MacLaine writes a book about her prior-life menopause as an Egyptian princess, or Britney Spears stars in a made-for-menopause DVD, *Can't Wait to Get Hot All Over.* Condoleezza Rice will claim she was going through hers during the war in Iraq.

After six months or so, figure on some backlash: Liza Minnelli takes accidental estrogen overdose. Or Swift Boat Veterans Out for Blood claim menopause overrated, unpatriotic.

If media exposure can make a celebrity out of menopause, imagine what a little public awareness might do for involuntary urine retention. The prostate is the most misunderstood, mispronounced gland in the male body. (The people who call it the "prostrate" are the same people who call nuclear "nucular.") When asked, "Where is it?" nine out of ten men answer, "Down there." The tenth will venture a guess. "It's what the doctor is looking for when he holds your balls and asks you to cough." How big is it? "Uh . . . dunno. It's either the size of a marble or a golf ball or a baseball." (Men like to think of their inner body parts as sporting goods. Women imagine produce.)

What does the prostate do? Nobody's sure. It either makes sperm, stores sperm, or ejaculates sperm. What is prostate trouble? It's when you want to pee but you can't pee. It's also why you have to have the aisle seat in a theater. (Why are men so ignorant about their bodies in general and their penises in particular? First they go to all the trouble of giving them names, and then they don't even want to get to know them!)

Only excruciating pain and the fear of exploding get their attention. Then they want to know. Then they'll see a doctor. Only then, when the doctor inserts his index finger in their rectum to palpate the swollen gland, do they learn where the prostate is. Only then do they find out that the gland, which has enlarged to the size of a hockey puck, is obstructing the flow of urine from their bladder, which is now the size of a basketball.

Only when they are under local anesthesia and see the surgeon coming straight at them brandishing a six-foot periscope mounted with a bayonet will they develop a healthy respect for the prostate. Its swelling will be celebrated as a middle-age rite of passage. There will be chants and drumbeats.

Maybe then the prostate will come out of the closet and take its rightful place in the pantheon of male parts, along with potbellies and hairy backs. There could be prostate chat rooms, prostate support groups, prostate reading clubs, e-dating, maybe even prostate pinups. Perhaps a movie called *Saddle Sore* about two cowboys with prostate trouble. This could be a hard sell. Call in George Clooney.

Baby Talk

- ❏ Abu
- ❏ Google
- ❏ Nano
- ❏ Mosh
- ❏ Bling
- ❏ Blang

- ❏ Eminem
- ❏ Bla bla
- ❏ Blog
- ❏ Uggs
- ❏ Duh
- ❏ Hip hop

- ❏ Su do ku
- ❏ Geek
- ❏ Imam
- ❏ Fatwa
- ❏ Dude
- ❏ Dubai

First Words

❑ Gotta get up.

❑ Everything hurts.

❑ We should remember to do that more often.

❑ What's the weather like?

❑ My bladder is bursting.

❑ What a night I had!

❑ What a dream I had!

❑ What a day I've got!

❑ I didn't sleep a wink.

❑ Coffee!

❑ Other ....

Teething

DEAD

GROUND DOWN
FROM STRESS

DEAD AND GONE

RECEDING GUMS

CAP

BONDED

BRIDGE

IMPLANT

GOLD CROWN

MINE

PULLED

Teething Toys

- ❑ Fork tine
- ❑ Matchbook cover
- ❑ Corner of 3 x 5 card
- ❑ Pointy fingernail
- ❑ Pine needle

- ❑ Toothpick
- ❑ Stim-U-Dent
- ❑ Dental floss
- ❑ Whitening strips
- ❑ Bite plate

MIDDLE-AGED

FLOSS

I Get Cranky: A Stress Test

(A score of 15 makes you best-stressed)

When the scale says you've gained weight, do you

❑ Recommit to your diet (1)

❑ Run around the room and weigh yourself again (2)

❑ Go get something to eat (3)

When you can't swipe your credit card the right way, do you

❑ Laugh it off and try again (1)

❑ Revert to cash (2)

❑ Suffer feelings of shame and fears of premature senility (3)

When you have to remain seated after the plane lands, do you

❑ Sit patiently and keep on hydrating (1)

❑ Turn on your cell phone and tell the whole world you've arrived (2)

❑ Stand up, open the storage bin, and make people hate you (3)

When you are driving behind someone who is obeying the speed limit, do you

❑ Pop in a Tibetan relaxation disc (1)

❑ Imagine yourself banging repeatedly into his bumper (2)

❑ Bang repeatedly into his bumper (3)

When your cell phone dies, do you

❑ Welcome the opportunity to shut up for a change (1)

❑ Open its little face and yell at it (2)

❑ Turn your anger inward and give yourself an autoimmune disease (3)

AM I SMILING…

or is it gas?

Q. *Where does intestinal gas come from?*

A. Gastroenterologists divide flatulents into two basic groups: Aerophagics (APs), from the Greek "air swallowers," and Intestinal Producers (IPs), people who manufacture their own internal air. APs tend to be nervous individuals who gulp excessive amounts of air (oxygen, nitrogen, and hydrogen) while talking and eating, drinking, smoking, chewing gum, or sucking breath fresheners. This swallowed air, along with the air that naturally occurs in staple foods such as Diet Cokes and Dairy Queens, lies in the stomach awaiting one of two possible fates: it may be brought up as a burp or expelled as gas. Which way it goes is a function of individual intestinal motility. Flatologists estimate that 50 to 70 percent of all the gas in the digestive tract comes from swallowed air. The remaining 30 to 50 percent is produced in the lower intestine during the fermenting process, called digestion. The resulting gases are expelled rectally. They are the ones that people try to blame on Labrador retrievers or on mice decomposing in the walls.

Q. *How can I tell if I'm primarily an Aerophagic or an Intestinal Producer?*

A. An informal, though quite reliable, determination can be made nasally: if the odor is aggressively paleolithic, you're an Intestinal Producer. If greater accuracy is desired, numerical readings can be taken. Research flatologist Dr. Michael Levitt was the first qualified person to insert a tube into the rectum and measure chemical gases.

Leftover holding area

Q. *What is intestinal gas made of?*

A. Leftovers. As a partially digested dinner moves out of the stomach and through the small intestine, little fingerlike projections called "villi" suck out the nutrients the body needs. What remains arrives at the portals of the ileocecal valve. This under-appreciated one-way valve is a triumph of waste management. No matter what, it keeps waste from reversing direction. Once the waste is safely deposited in the large intestine, bacteria known as "intestinal flora" turn the undigested sugars into gas.

Q. *Why do people pass more wind as they get older?*

A. Diet. Grains, green and leafy vegetables, fruits, beans, and Amstel Light are the staple ingredients of low-fat and high-fart diets. But probably the more common cause of excessive mid-life flatulence is a condition called "lactose intolerance" caused by an insufficient amount of the enzyme lactase, which breaks down the lactose in Nacho Fiestas and Chunky Monkey, making them easy to digest. As a result of this enzyme deficiency, the amount of undigested sugars in waste matter increases. It is estimated that up to one half of middle-aged people suffer from lactose intolerance, whether they know it or not. If they don't know it, someone should tell them.

Q. *What gives gas its distinctive odor?*

A. Methane makes the difference between low-octane aerophagic and premium high-test. Without methane, gas can never be important.

Q. *What determines what kind of noise gas makes?*

A. The laws of physics determine whether passed gas sounds like the squeal of a sneaker on a gym floor or the Fourth of July. As with a pinched or released balloon, the sound of flatus is related to the volume of gas, the distance of the gas from the sphincter, and the tension in the sphincter itself. For example, an SBD (the much admired Silent But Deadly) is colonically based, has traveled a short way, and has met with little resistance. Given all the variables, the tonal and stylistic possibilities of gas are virtually infinite.

Q. *How much gas does the average middle-aged person expel each day?*

A. About 17.5 ounces (plus or minus 12).

Q. *How can my body tell the difference between gas and solid matter?*

A. The rectum can think. When the rectum dilates, it transmits the appropriate urge to the brain. Usually.

Q. *How long after a meal does the average middle-aged person start passing wind?*

A. Intestinal transit varies from two to six hours, which is why middle-aged people like to leave a dinner party by ten.

I Grow Hair

Color: ....   Real color: ....

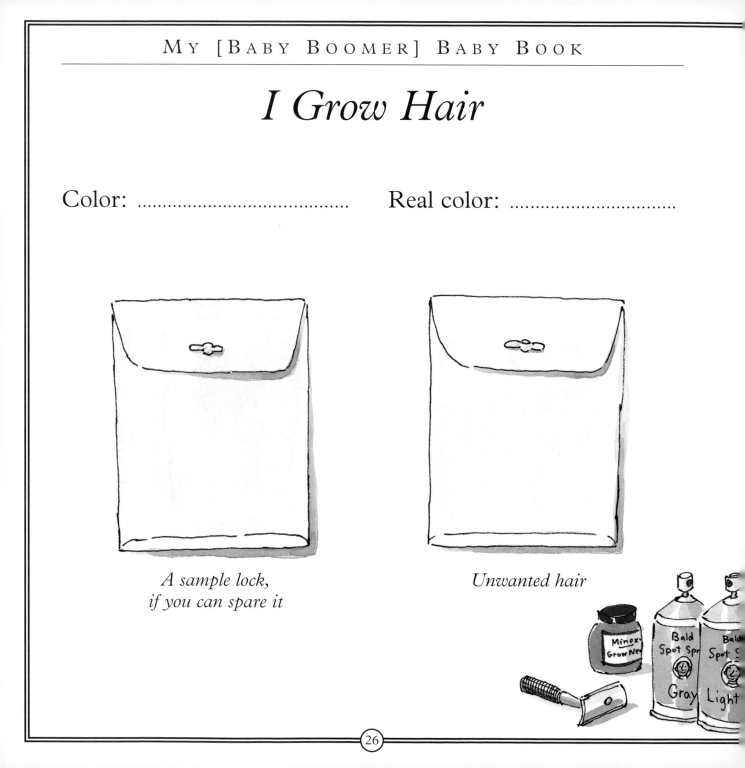

*A sample lock,
if you can spare it*

Unwanted hair

The Seven Stages of Men's Hair Loss

- ❑ Tries Propecia

- ❑ Dyes remaining hairs mahogany

- ❑ Parts hair closer to ear and arranges strands in snail-like pattern on anterior of head

- ❑ Tries hair plugs

- ❑ Grows beard

- ❑ Shaves head

- ❑ Wears baseball cap backward

The Seven Stages of Women's Hair Coloring

- ❑ Pulls out gray hairs

- ❑ Tries henna rinse

- ❑ Has hair highlighted

- ❑ Dyes hair original color

- ❑ Decides to let it go gray

- ❑ Has hair lowlighted *and* highlighted

- ❑ Dyes it champagne blond

I Dress Myself

Fashion Firsts for Big Boys

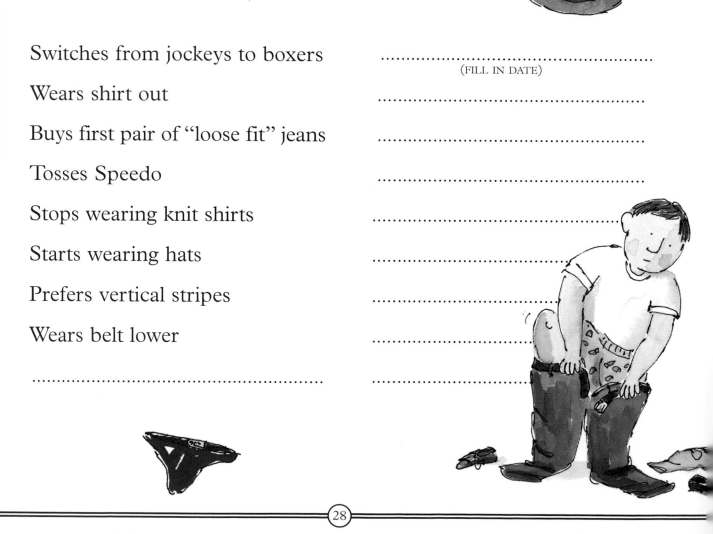

Switches from jockeys to boxers ....

(FILL IN DATE)

Wears shirt out ....

Buys first pair of "loose fit" jeans ....

Tosses Speedo ....

Stops wearing knit shirts ....

Starts wearing hats ....

Prefers vertical stripes ....

Wears belt lower ....

....

Fashion Firsts for Big Girls

Switches from heels to flats ....
(FILL IN DATE)

Doesn't tuck in shirts ....

Buys first jeans with elastic waist ....

Tosses bikini ....

Stops wearing spandex ....

Favors scarves and turtlenecks ....

Prefers pastels ....

Stops wearing belts ....

....

My Primary Caregivers

HAIRDRESSER: ....TEL: ....

INTERNIST: ....TEL: ....

PODIATRIST: ....TEL: ....

UROLOGIST: ....TEL: ....

NUTRITIONIST: ....TEL: ....

NEUROLOGIST: ....TEL: ....

PSYCHOLOGIST: ....TEL: ....

PROCTOLOGIST: ....TEL: ....

GYNECOLOGIST: ....TEL: ....

DERMATOLOGIST: ....TEL: ....

RADIOLOGIST: ....TEL: ....

REFLEXOLOGIST: ....   TEL: ....

OPHTHALMOLOGIST: ....TEL: ....

RHEUMATOLOGIST: ....TEL: ....

ENDOCRINOLOGIST: ....TEL: ....

ELECTROLOGIST: ....TEL: ....

PERIODONTIST: ....TEL: ....

OTOLARYNGOLOGIST: ....TEL: ....

GASTROENTEROLOGIST: ....TEL: ....

PSYCHOPHARMACOLOGIST: ....TEL: ....

MANICURIST: ....TEL: ....

FINANCIAL ADVISER: ....TEL: ....

ASTROLOGER: ....TEL: ....

PERSONAL TRAINER: ....TEL: ....

LAWYER: ....TEL: ....

PSYCHIC: ....TEL: ....

MASSEUSE: ....TEL: ....

COSMETIC SURGEON: ....TEL: ....

COMPUTER TUTOR: ....TEL: ....

PILATES INSTRUCTOR: ....TEL: ....

YOGA INSTRUCTOR: ....TEL: ....

ACUPUNCTURIST: ....TEL: ....

HERBALIST: ....TEL: ....

COLORIST: ....TEL: ....

LIFE COACH: ....TEL: ....

OTHER: ....TEL: ....

INTRODUCING SOLID FOODS

10,459 B.C. • The Evolutionary Diet. Early person's diet consists mostly of takeout—nuts, berries, roots, and tubers.

Alternate Creationist Diet. All the fruit you can eat, except apples.

The Savage Special. The eating of red meat has a special allure for early persons not concerned with political correctness or arterial plaque. Tribal people ascribe magical homeopathic qualities to eating free-range meat. Eating tiger makes a person brave and strong. Rabbit makes one timid. "You are what you eat" is taken literally.

7000 B.C. • The Rise of Bread. The innocent age of hunting and gathering is brought to an abrupt end by the development of agriculture in the Neolithic period, specifically the cultivation of grain, and the subsequent discovery of beer, corn chips, and the resting pulse. The appearance of the first fat person.

A.D. 250 • The Romans Invent Bulimia.

1894 • The First Hershey Bar.

1900–1930 • THE AGE OF ANALYSIS. The seven basic food groups are taught in the public schools, but people can only remember "green and leafy vegetables." The discovery of the calorie reveals a causal link between eating too much and weighing too much. More people get fat.

1930S • THE DAWN OF DIETING. The first diets were predicated on the theory of rapid transit: the faster the food moves through the body, the smaller the weight gain. The Grapefruit-and-an-Enema Diet attracts few adherents. The Duchess of Windsor is the first to link wealth and thinness. Even more people get fat.

1949 • THE CLEAN PLATE CLUB OF AMERICA. Membership reaches an all-time high.

1950–1960 • THE DARK AGES OF DIETING. Pizza is named the eighth food group. Bacon is thought to contain important minerals. Sara Lee says, "Let them eat cake." More and more people get fatter and fatter.

1963 • THE FIRST DIET SODA: TaB.

1980–1990 • THE ENLITENMENT. Cholesterol is discovered and counted. Polys are unsaturated. Stouffer says, "Let there be lite," and there is lite and lo cal and no cal. Headmistress Jean Harris shoots diet doctor Herman Tarnower.

1993 • OPRAH STARTS DIETING.

1994 • THE GREAT DEPRESSION. Government studies show that dieting rarely results in permanent weight loss (the Yo-Yo Ma factor). Liposuction and the dawn of Invasive Dieting.

2002 • AL ROKER HAS FIRST CELEBRITY GASTRIC BYPASS SURGERY.

2003–4 • THE REAL ESTATE DIET BOOK CRAZE. Desperate, the overweight invest in diet books that come from places where only rich, thin people live: South Beach, the Hamptons, Sonoma, the Gold Coast. People continue to be as big as McMansions.

2005 • OBESITY BECOMES THE NEW FAT.

2006 • X-TREME STARVATION. Scientists discover that a high-nutrient 890 calorie per day diet results in significant weight loss, slows aging, and may not make life worth living.

2007 • THE MILLENNIUM OF PERMANENT WEIGHT LOSS. Surgery replaces willpower. The primitive practices of liposuction and stomach stapling are abandoned in favor of organectomy, the removal of all nonessential and redundant inner body parts. Gall bladder (1 ounce); spleen (10 ounces); a kidney (5 ounces); a lung (16 ounces); tonsils and adenoids (1½ ounces); appendix (½ ounce). Total permanent weight loss: 2 pounds, 2 ounces. Hey! It's a start.

My Playpen

1. Visor microphone
2. Microwave radar
3. Dashboard ionizer
4. GPS navigation system
5. Climate control navigation
6. Satellite radio receiver
7. MP3 player
8. Mini-refrigerator
9. Hands-free car phone
10. Seat belt tension sensor
11. Ventilating seat fan
12. TV/DVD player
13. Good-Vibes neck massager

Toilet Training

(Check where appropriate)

Make public announcement? Yes .... No ....

Door open? .... Door closed? ....

Take in cell phone? Yes .... No ....

Paper trained? Yes .... No ....

　　　Newspaper: .... Crossword puzzles: ....

　　　Magazine: .... Laptop: ....

　　　Catalogs: ....

　　　　　Victoria's Secret .... L.L.Bean ....

Look? Yes .... No ....

Engage in self-praise? Yes .... No ....

Make public announcement? Yes .... No ....

My Bedtime Ritual

- ❏ No caffeine after noon
- ❏ No fluids after 8 p.m.
- ❏ Brush and floss
- ❏ Empty bladder
- ❏ Get in bed
- ❏ Set alarm
- ❏ Watch something
- ❏ Empty bladder
- ❏ Have insomnia
- ❏ Watch anything
- ❏ Empty bladder
- ❏ Have insomnia
- ❏ Read something
- ❏ Empty bladder
- ❏ Turn off alarm
- ❏ Have insomnia
- ❏ Turn clock to wall
- ❏ Cry out to a higher being
- ❏ Nuke a pizza
- ❏ Pop a sleeping pill

Favorite Nursery Rhymes

This little piggy has a bunion,
This little piggy's ingrown,
This little piggy's arthritic,
This little piggy's all bone,
And this little piggy cries,
"My feet are killing me,"
All the way home.

Rock-a-bye ovum in a petrie dish.
When you divide you'll look like a fish.
When you grow up, nobody will know
That you weren't conceived
        while in utero.

Mrs. Dumpty sat on a wall.
Mrs. Dumpty had a great fall.
Osteoporosis and low estrogen
Shattered her hip, so they put in a pin.

Old King Saud
Had an emirate proud,
Of his emirate proud was he.
He had so much gas
(Now I hate to be crass, but)
He blew down
    his fiddlers three.

It's raining, it's pouring,
This could be global warming.
But what do I care,
I'm not a polar bear,
So I don't find it alarming.

One, two—can't reach my shoe.
Three, four—can't get off the floor.
Five, six—what a fix.
Seven, eight—must have put on
some weight.
Nine, ten—a big fat hen.

Mary has some dental floss;
She keeps it with her so . . .
When shish kebab sticks in her teeth,
The lamb is sure to go.

Jack and Jill
Went through the mill
Of sexual dysfunction;
Jack's fell down,
Jill broke his crown
Without the least compunction.

My Friends

Friends I work with ....

Friends I work out with ....

Friends I've outgrown ....

Friends I'd go on vacation with ....

Friends I went on vacation with ....

Friends on speed dial..

Friends on the Season's Greetings list ....

Friends I keep promising to get together with but never do....................

Friends who are nice, but I don't like them ....

Friends I e-mail ....

Virtual friends

❏ Katie Couric
❏ Dr. Sanjay Gupta
❏ Oprah
❏ Dr. Phil
❏ Ellen DeGeneres

Likes and Dislikes

LIKE: Caller ID
DISLIKE: Out-of-area callers

DISLIKE: College reunions
LIKE: Looking better than everyone else

LIKE: When the FDA approves a fat substitute
DISLIKE: When further scientific studies prove the fat substitute causes cancer
LIKE: When the so-called scientific studies arc shown to be faulty

LIKE: Telling my dreams
DISLIKE: Listening to other people's dreams

LIKE: Paying $20 for a digital camera on eBay
DISLIKE: Paying $40 to have it shipped

DISLIKE: When construction workers whistle
DISLIKE: When they don't

LIKE: When nobody notices my face-lift
DISLIKE: When nobody notices my face-lift

LIKE:..
DISLIKE:..

My Favorite Expressions

Where did I put my glasses?
That's totally awesome.
Dressing on the side, please.
It works for me.

They're not in my pocket.
It's a win/win situation.
I need some closure.
Omigod.

Has anyone seen my glasses?
It is what it is.
I hardly ever watch TV.
Oh, puh-leeze.

Maybe I left them by the phone.
No problema.
She's had some work done.
I'm on hold.

I had them just a minute ago.
What's your e-mail?
60's the new 50.
Life is short.

Your glasses are on your forehead.
Are you wireless?
At the end of the day
I'm good to go.

I CAN READ

Obituary reading begins in middle age and is considered a normal developmental stage. There are those who argue that this new habit represents the maturing person's first concession to the possibility of mortality. They are wrong. A mature person doesn't concede a damn thing. Death is not inevitable. Death is what happens to people who don't take good enough care of themselves. Death is a mistake for which we have only ourselves to blame. Death is what happens when people refuse to profit from the obituaries of others.

Relatively speaking, our parents knew very little about death prevention. And what they knew was often based on ignorance and superstition. They didn't know cows could kill. They didn't know about the body-mind connection. They couldn't tell brain-dead from really dead. They didn't even have wellness —just health. As a result they tended to accept the inevitability of their own mortality. Because we are well enough informed about the kinds of lifestyles, habits, and states of mind that invite death, Boomers can be the first generation to learn to take responsibility for avoiding it.

Learning how to read the obituaries can add years to your life. A quick, cowardly glance at the headlines, just to reassure yourself that everyone who has died is at least a decade or two older than you, only brings temporary relief. To keep death permanently at bay, obituaries must be read thoroughly, studied thoughtfully, and deconstructed strictly. The question to keep in mind is not "What did the deceased die of?" but "What did the deceased do wrong that resulted in his or her failure to maintain perpetual wellness?"

Cancer is not a cause of death; smoking is. Heart attacks are not a cause of death; eating fried eggs, hash browns, and bacon every morning is.

Obituary writers, perhaps out of some warped notion of good taste, give us precious little hard information to go on, preferring soothing euphemisms like "natural causes" and "after a long illness" to explicit accusations and I-told-you-so's. Nevertheless, an expert obituary reader can make a "blame" diagnosis from the kind of evidence that amateurs would be inclined to overlook as boring and irrelevant.

Sometimes you have to read all the way to the apparently inno-cent tag line to get to the blame behavior. "Mr. So-and-So was a lifelong resident of Los Angeles."

In this case death was caused by the deceased's stubborn insistence upon living with free radicals in a city where the air quality index is set permanently on "unacceptable."

"Mrs. So-and-So died at her winter home in Boca Raton after a long illness." Melanoma. Not using sunblock. Or, if she did use sunblock, not using a high enough SPF. There are *explanations* for dying, but no more excuses.

Sometimes an obituary offers multiple choices: "Mr. What's-His-Name, a lawyer with the New York Stock Exchange, traveled frequently to Asia." Can you name at least three potential blame behaviors? Mr. What's-His-Name may have died because he did not learn to control his stress levels with biofeedback and positive imaging. Or he might have crossed his legs on an airplane, which, especially during long trips at high altitudes, can cause a fatal deep vein thrombosis. Or he might have neglected to get a flu shot before traveling to China where he contracted bird flu as a result of eating undercooked poultry. It hardly matters which one did him in. Deconstructed is deconstructed.

Some obits are a challenge even for the experts. A case in point is the syndicated TV aerobics instructor, dead at the age of 45. He suffered his first and only heart attack while reading an unsensational novel in the shade of a recently pruned tree. Even his closest friend, quoted in the obituary, could not identify the blame behavior. "He never smoked. He never drank. He took his daily doses of human growth factor, fiber, and folic acid and never ate farmed fish. He was on a fat-free diet. He meditated. He wore a surgical mask on airplanes. He took a gram of aspirin every day. He rode a bike. He swam two miles a day. He consulted with his doctor and had a stress test before embarking on any exercise program. He was a frequent flosser. He read *Prevention* magazine. He had achieved his target pulse. He had balanced his polarities. He had a crystal. I don't get it."

He was too self-involved. God doesn't like narcissists.

I CAN COUNT

Hello. You have reached 1-800-RAGE, the virtual waiting room of Digital Doc, P.C. Due to the usually high volume of entitled-feeling sick people and the shortage of doctors who are willing to put up with HMOs, insurance forms, and Medicare payments, you may experience some delays. Please listen to the following options so that we may better serve you.

For English, press **1**.

Para Español, oprimer **ABC 2**.

If you are a physician or a pharmacist, or if this is a true medical emergency—you are unconscious or you have lost the use of all four limbs and your nose—press **DEF 3**.

(If you even thought *of passing yourself off as a physician or a pharmacist, press* **GHI 4** *.)*

To make an appointment, press **JKL 5**.

"You have reached the appointment office. I am either away from my desk or on another call. Please leave a message after the beep and someone will call you back."

(Do not press 0; we're on to you.)

In the event that you have actually secured an appointment for a time that does not exceed your life expectancy and want directions to our office, press .

"You have reached the directions office. I am either away from my desk, on another call, or lost. It is also possible that there are no directions, no desk, and no me—just a recording. Are you pissed off yet?"

(If you are gnashing your teeth, press **1** *. If you are saying the F-word, press* **2** *.)*

To refill a prescription, press **7** .

"You have reached the prescription desk of—'*Blah, blah, blah, blah, blah, blah. . .*'

"There is nobody here to hear you say '*blah, blah, blah, blah, blah.*' Please leave your name, your mother's maiden name, your insurance identification and Social Security numbers, the number of the prescription you wish to have refilled, the phone number of your pharmacy, your credit card number, and the last three numbers of the code that appears on the back of the card, and no one will be with you shortly."

To return to the main menu, press **1** **3** .

For all other inquiries, please stay on the line and your call will be answered in the order in which it was received. Current estimated waiting time is tomorrow.

Meanwhile, if you'd like to listen to "The Flight of the Bumblebee" over and over again, press **8** . For Beethoven's Ninth, press **9** .

If you are calling from a rotary phone, hang up, take two aspirin, and dial 911.

Sex?

(Check one)

❏ Yes   ❏ No   ❏ Can't remember

Middle-aged sex is much more exciting than:

❏ The moist, breathless, throbbing coital passions of youth.

❏ Sneaking into the movies as a senior citizen.

❏ Watching grass grow.

❏ ....

I would have sex more often, but:

❏ I keep forgetting how much I like it.

❏ The foreplay is too much work.

❏ Nobody asks.

❏ ....

A good time to have sex is:

❑ Spontaneously, right after I've checked and answered all my e-mail.

❑ During commercials.

❑ When the kids have left for college.

❑ When we're both awake.

❑ ....

Things you might say while having sex:

❑ Ooooo*ohh!* That's my bad knee.

❑ Is that you or me?

❑ I can't *get* in that position.

❑ Don't roll on the cats!

❑ I'm turning off the TV.

❑ ....

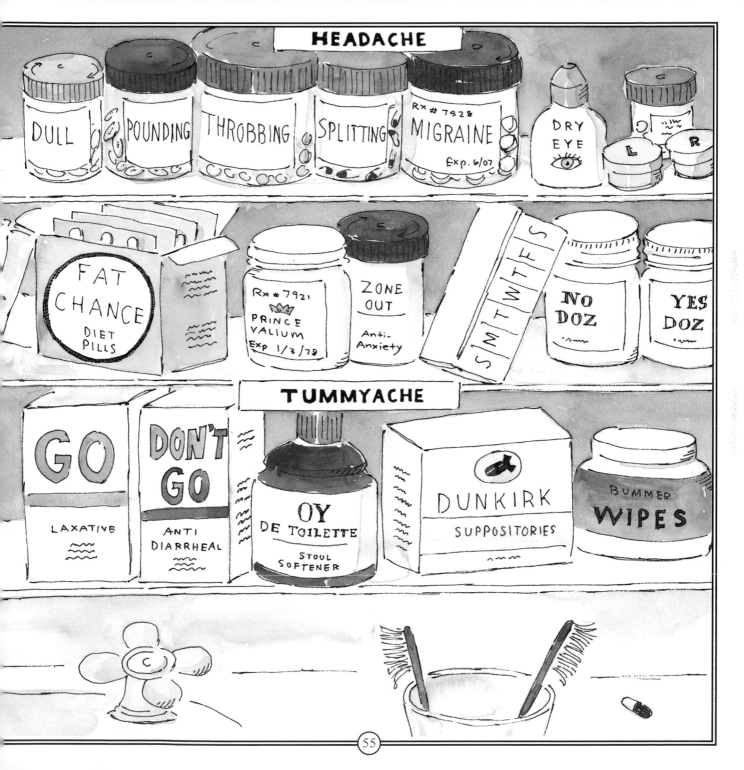

I FORGET

After the age of 30, the brain loses about 10,000 neurons a day. These nerve cells tend to take the car keys with them and leave important things behind, like the words and music to the Mickey Mouse Club theme song. This process is called "forgetting." It does not help to wear a hat.

During a typical 24-hour period, 10,000 neurons can carry off with them the multiplication tables through times 12, the names of all the state capitals, and every joke you've ever heard, including the last one. It is possible to resupply the brain with neurons and thereby offset the loss by increasing the flow of high-octane information into the brain, but it's a zero sum game. By the time an individual reaches the age of 45, it takes two hours of Mandarin instruction and a game of chess with a grand master to make up for a single day of neuron loss. Most people would rather rent a video.

There are two basic kinds of forgetting: losing one's train of thought and losing the passengers on one's train of thought. Losing one's train is caused by a sudden mass defection of neurons. One moment you're moving purposefully toward your destination. The next, you're standing stupidly in the doorway, mentally derailed. *"What did I come in here for?"* Dental floss? A tissue? Nail clippers? You haven't the foggiest. Nothing. Nada. This kind of memory loss brings one to the edge of existential despair, gives one a nauseating glimpse of the abyss, and stuns one with the blunt purposelessness of life. *"Why am I here?"* Why, indeed.

Thinking about it doesn't help. Occasionally, through reenactment, one is able to grab hold of the caboose, thereby rescuing one's train in mid-abyss. You retrace your steps, assuming, of course, that you can remember what it was you were doing immediately before you forgot what it was you came in for. You do. You go to the sink to retrieve the coffee cup and spoon you had been using moments earlier, before the twinkie blackout. You pour a pretend cup of coffee, spoon in a bit of pretend sugar, and pretend-stir it. You pick up the paper and can't see the words. Then you stride purposefully, triumphantly into the next room to get your glasses. You feel grateful that no one is home to witness this embarrassing charade.

You worry. Is this aimless wandering a normal, run-of-the-mill senior moment or is it the beginning of you-know-what? You call a friend for reassurance. You tell her your story. She says the same thing happens to her all the time. You feel better. Then you worry: maybe both of you have you-know-what.

At least losing one's train is almost always a private act. Losing the passengers on the train, however, is invariably a public act and therefore potentially more humiliating. Passenger loss is characterized by the annoying yet tantalizing feeling that a word—most often a name—is right on the tip of one's tongue. In fact, it is not. The surname– or punch line–bearing neuron has already leapt off the tongue and is airborne.

Just a moment ago, a roomful of people were hanging on your every word. Now they are held hostage while

you grope for the lost word as if it were a dropped contact lens. "Wait a second! Hold it! Don't anybody move! I had it just a second ago. He's a famous actor. First name starts with a B. Or an F. You know who I mean. He's a character actor. Plays bad guys. His name goes like this—Boom. Ba Boom. First name, one syllable; second, two. I think. C'mon. You know this guy. He's always squinting and he walks kinda like this. . . ."

It is considered rude to forget in public. Forgetting, like sneezing, coughing, and burping, is an unexpected, unwanted intrusion into the lives of innocent bystanders. Although forgetting is one of the few bodily emissions that does not make its own exit noise, it is invariably accompanied by other behaviors that polite people find at least as offensive. Straining at remembering should be a private act. If forgetting in public does occur, just keep talking. Act as if nothing has happened. It's no big deal. You're just losing your mind. Wave bye-bye.

See How I've Grown★

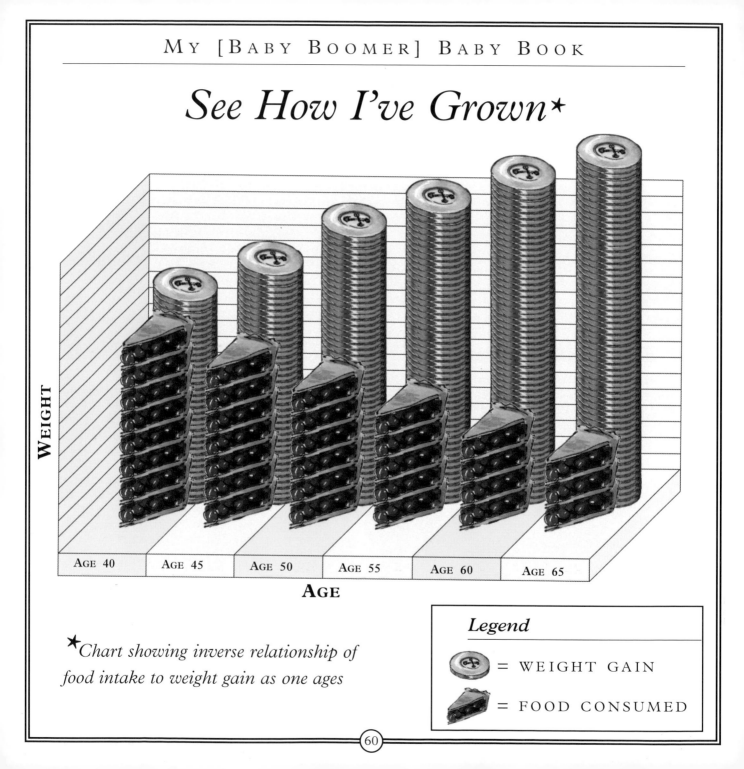

WEIGHT

| AGE 40 | AGE 45 | AGE 50 | AGE 55 | AGE 60 | AGE 65 |

AGE

★*Chart showing inverse relationship of food intake to weight gain as one ages*

Legend

= WEIGHT GAIN

= FOOD CONSUMED

See What I've Grown

- ☐ ....
- ☐ ....
- ☐ *Eye flaps*
- ☐ *Chin hairs*
- ☐ *Turkey neck*
- ☐ *Liver spots*
- ☐ *Dewlaps*
- ☐ *Elbow flaps*
- ☐ *Swag arm*
- ☐ *Pendulous breasts*
- ☐ *Pot belly*
- ☐ *Piles*
- ☐ *Love handles*
- ☐ *Enlarged prostate*
- ☐ *Knee flaps*
- ☐ *Sock line*
- ☐ *Varicose veins*
- ☐ ....
- ☐ *Corns*
- ☐ ....

I TAKE MY MEDICINE

If you are afflicted by fear of aging, or would like to live on indefinitely in a suspended state of perpetual middle age—think Barbara Walters —you may want to ask your doctor if Immortalis is right for you. (Remember, only a doctor can tell you if you have an aging affliction.)

Immortalis is a prescription *clock blocker.* All blockers work in similar ways, but only a clock blocker effectively turns back your chronometer, reversing the mitrochondrial mutations that are responsible for aging. One time-release capsule, taken every morning, will arrest the aging process for 24 hours if used in conjunction with a program of diet, exercise, cosmetic and reconstructive surgery, gene splicing, tissue cloning, chelation, and sleeping upside down in the freezer.

Immortalis is not for everyone. Do not take Immortalis if you have a thawing problem. (Remember, only a doctor can tell you if you have a thawing problem.) Side effects may include light-headedness, no-headedness, freezer burn, and wishing you were dead.

WARNING: Age is more than a number; it's a risk factor that should not be ignored.

My Imaginary Friend

My Personality

(Check where appropriate)

I am the kind of person who . . .

- ❑ Carries a water bottle everywhere
- ❑ Can't wait for Armageddon
- ❑ Likes speed dating
- ❑ Eats vegan
- ❑ Really doesn't care how fat I get
- ❑ Would take performance-enhancing drugs in a red hot minute
- ❑ Wants to kill when I hear gangsta rap
- ❑ Feng shuied the entire house, and the plants died
- ❑ Can't relax (not even with votive candles and aromatherapy)

❑ Is just beginning to appreciate my parents

❑ Would never sign a prenup

❑ Doesn't know what half the icons on my computer mean

❑ Is ambivalent about buying a hybrid

❑ Is never going to retire

My issues are . . .

❑ Aging parents

❑ Aging children

❑ Aging

❑ Deer in my garden

❑ Empty nest euphoria

❑ Delusions of immortality

❑ Resistance to global warming

❑ Simple exhaustion

❑ Other ....

I have . . .

- ❏ ADD
- ❏ ADHD
- ❏ ACDC
- ❏ ABCD
- ❏ OCD

- ❏ HBO
- ❏ GPS
- ❏ CNN
- ❏ ESPN
- ❏ ESP

I smile when . . .

- ❏ I get positive feedback
- ❏ I get a rebate
- ❏ I'm full

I get overstimulated when . . .

- ❏ I'm on my second Cosmo
- ❏ I watch the playoffs
- ❏ I stay up past my bedtime

I laugh when . . .

❑ I'm feeling defensive

❑ I watch Comedy Central

❑ I'm tickled

I cry when . . .

❑ I suffer feelings of low self-esteem

❑ The cowboy gets on the horse and rides off into the sunset

❑ I need a change

❑ Other...

My fears are . . .

❑ Rejection

❑ Humiliation

❑ Abandonment

❑ Other...

I GO TO SCHOOL

The No-Adult-Left-Behind School of Continuing Education
Fall Catalog

The Elder Hostile Movement

In this course we will examine the many
ways human beings throughout history
have treated their elders, such as
worshipping them, institutionalizing
them, killing and eating them, putting them
on ice floes, calling them "senior citizens," and giving them discounts.

Advanced Spiritual Development Workshop

You've got your mantra, you've met your angels,
and you've experienced at least one past-life regression.
You are now ready to accomplish the ultimate in spirituality—
haunting. 13 sessions. Bring a sheet to the first class.

I Remember Moi Moi

It's time to get going on your memoirs—something for Knopf or maybe a short piece for *The New Yorker*. People have been telling you for years that you have a way with words. You, too, have been feeling there is something inside you that needs to come out. We'll teach you how to get it out and on paper.

Luddite Support Group

Meet and socialize weekly with other middle-aged people who have had it with technology. Activities will include writing snail mail to one another; looking up words in a paper dictionary; and talking to one another on phones that plug into walls. $25 additional fee for field trips to auctions and department stores.

Residential Real Estate (Appraisal and Sales)

A lucrative career in real estate is a popular choice for the woman with a divorce and a BA in something useless, like philosophy or American lit. If you don't mind driving around on weekends, this introductory course will increase your odds of finding a husband— usually a recently separated one—who is looking for a charming Cotswold-style cottage to rent while his wife is busy dating her lawyer.

AutoCAD

Women like computer nerds with plenty of RAM. Learn how to be the master of your 3-D domain, issue commands, pump up your drafting skills, and navigate your toolbar. Prerequisite skills: Uploading, Downloading, Inputting, and Outputting.

Genealogy 101

Google your roots. Everybody else is. Do you want to know who you are and where your ancestors came from? Did they work for Al Capone or Al Jazeera? Were any of them evildoers or just black sheep? Learn how to use the Internet to spy on yourself. Why should the FBI, the CIA, the NSA, and the Mormon Tabernacle Choir know more about you than you do?

Evangelical Science

Did the apple just happen to drop on Newton's head or did God throw it on purpose? Is gravity really a law? What if we are held in place by an intelligent designer with Krazy Glue? In this 10-week course we will rigorously explore the relative "truthiness" of gravity and other so-called theories.

Evolution? Are you serious!?

Why . . .

Do gums recede?

Do strangers half my age call me by my first name?

Don't I recognize the people in People anymore?

Didn't I make a list of my credit card numbers?

Why . . .

Do some people take up two parking spaces?

Are people my age running the world?

Can't I understand computer instructions when
they're supposed to be written for dummies?

Won't my children get married?

Why . . .

Don't they outlaw SUVs?

Do fingernails get ridges?

Is it that the phone doesn't ring for days, and then
all of a sudden everybody calls at once?

Aren't I having more fun?

Why . . .

Don't they make cars with
bumpers anymore?

Does time speed up?

Don't I feel any older?

Is the sky blue?

I KNOW LEFT FROM RIGHT

Like adolescence, middle age is a time when the maturing individual undergoes radical changes: at the same time that the body thickens, the mind begins to veer to the right. People suddenly find themselves entertaining conservative opinions that bear an uncomfortable resemblance to the opinions of people they formerly laughed at and called "old geezers."

This process usually starts at about the age of 40—give or take a few stock options—and picks up steam in the next two decades, until the individual is totally right.

Nobody knows for sure what causes veering. It could be hormonal, like a growth spurt; or it could be the result of intelligent design; or it may be, as Darwinians suggest, that the desire to hold on to as much of one's stuff for as long as possible, while advising others to pull themselves up by their bootstraps, has survival value for the species.

The first few weeks can be unsettling. You will horrify yourself by beginning a sentence with the

LIBERAL CONSERVATIVE

20 yrs. 30 yrs. 40 yrs. 50 yrs. 60 yrs. 70 yrs. 80

phrase: "The trouble with those people is . . . Oops! Never mind." Alien thoughts will arise unbidden and invade your mind, causing confusion and doubt.

"What if the trickle down theory *does* have merit. Humm."

"How come they're searching me and not that guy in the turban? Uh-oh!"

"And, come to think of it, is it fair to tax people for dying?" For a while you will be able to keep these embarrassing thoughts to yourself. Then you won't.

The next stage is the most disconcerting. You will stand by helplessly as you involuntarily blurt out the unspeakable in loud Tourette's-like barks. "Screw the caribou!" "Guns don't kill!" "Bomb the bastards!" These outbursts will be followed by others, all of which you will wish to disown the minute they leave your mouth. Mercifully, the third and final stage of conservative rectitude is amnesia: you will forget that you weren't always right.

You are now completely comfortable with your new conservative self. It's so much easier to have zero tolerance than to wring your hands about the plight of people who should have figured out by now how to stand on their own two feet. You will actively enjoy being right about everything. Restaurants *are* too noisy. Taxes *are* too high. Parents *shouldn't* allow kids to put studs through their tongues. And you know what else? You know how the older generation always claims that the world is going to hell in a handbasket? Well, *this time*, it really is.

Welcome to Middle Age. Enjoy it. It comes just before Old Fart.

First Recognize Self

I Remember When . . .

A document was an official paper

Hot could burn you

Extraordinary rendition
   was a compliment

Same sex meant the
   same old missionary position

Only spiders had webs

The price point was the price

And 50 wasn't the new anything

A cell was for prisoners

Sopranos sang on stage

Super Nanny was Mary Poppins

A blue tooth was a dental emergency

Amazon meant a river in Brazil

Cookies were something you ate

Branding was for cattle

Plasma meant blood

WHEN I GROW UP

It is never too soon to consider what kind of a place you would most like to live in when you grow up. There are a number of independent senior citizen lifestyle models from which you may choose. Some come with nutritionists. Some have country clubs. Some have special outfits.

One of the most popular plans involves selling the house and buying a condo somewhere warm where everyone is about your own age. You will learn how to pronounce angina. (The accent is on the first syllable.) You will complain that people are dropping all around you like flies. You will not drive at night. You will wear a pastel running suit and eat dinner at 4:30. The children and grandchildren will come to visit over Christmas vacation.

A gated community is a good choice for the walking wealthy and for those who prefer aboveground interment. All visitors will be announced. Your Jacuzzi will be equipped with special grab bars. You will toot around in a golf cart in a perfectly manicured riffraff-free environment.

Another alternative, the extended care facility, promises to take care of you forever, no matter what, in exchange for all your assets, including the proceeds from the sale of your home. If you're healthy, you'll live in a town house, play golf or tennis, read great books in the library, fish in the freshly stocked trout stream, and eat meals prepared by a gourmet chef. If you get sick, you'll go to the facility's own luxury hospital. If you stay sick, you will go to their four-star nursing home. If you die, they get to keep your leftover money.

A third is the minimalist option: Don't sell the house. Tough it out alone. Stockpile frozen dinners. Continue paying for lawn maintenance. Tolerate the happy sounds of children at play. Wear an electronic necklace connected to a central switchboard, and be picked up off your own floor by a total stranger.

The Do-It-Yourself Retirement Colony is a popular alternative among latter-day hippies who have spent a lifetime resisting the increasing influence of corporate America in every aspect of human life, and will therefore be damned if they are going to let some Sun City–type developer who probably never wore Birkenstocks design them a so-called lifestyle. While an exemplary few such communities have been designed, built, and inhabited, most of them get bogged down in the talking stages.

"We should all pitch in and buy an inn, or maybe a summer camp in Colorado, or if that's too cold in the winter, maybe something somewhere farther south. Whatever, we've got to be on water, or at least near water. We'll live in the original cabins—we may have to winterize them—and eat in what used to be the camp's dining room. We should probably have a microwave or maybe even a kitchen in each cabin, just to assure some privacy. But we could share the bathrooms. Or maybe we'd build extra bathrooms. Maybe even one for each person. With a lock.

"But the most important thing is we'll pledge to take care of one another—no matter what. If, God forbid, you are confined to a wheelchair, I will push you. We'll all push you. We'll take turns. You'll never have to be cared for by strangers, unless for some reason we all want to go somewhere together— we have theater tickets and the lift on the van is broken—and we can't take you."

Or, you can be a burden. All of the above model senior citizen lifestyles are predicated on the counterintuitive belief that children should not have to take care of their elderly parents, at least not in person. And parents believe—with a devotion bordering on fanaticism—that they must not, under any circumstances, be a burden to their children.

Nonsense! Why not be a burden to them? They were a burden to you. Didn't you love them, feed them, and sing to them when they couldn't sleep? Didn't you take care of them when they were sick? Didn't you change their diapers? Didn't you do your very best, never mind how they happened to have turned out? And you don't want to be a burden to them? What are you—crazy? If not now, when?

Of course they should lead their own lives, although there's nothing wrong with the life you gave them. Who's stopping them? That doesn't mean you can't live their own lives with them. You'll need your own suite.

At a time when the American family is breaking down, when the foster care system pays grandparents to take care of their grandchildren, you are offering your services free. You are the embodiment of family values. You are the extended family everybody's been whining about for the last two decades. Your children and your children's children need you. Why stubbornly insist upon maintaining your precious independence when someone else can do it for you? Does it really surprise you that life requires yet another sacrifice from you? Go ahead. Be a burden.

MY HOROSCOPE

ARIES

THE RAM
MARCH 21–APRIL 19

You are pure energy and always on the move. With your ruling planet in Mars and your third mortgage in the first house, you are unlikely to retire to the Sun Belt and start sending your children boxed fruit anytime soon. Hiking in Patagonia is a real possibility for next spring. So are dental implants.

TAURUS

THE BULL
APRIL 20–MAY 20

You are stubborn, conservative, deliberate, and full of it—the last person in your crowd to give up cigarettes and the first to complain about secondary smoke. Still, you are loyal, dependable, and generous to a fault and would give away your upgrades if they let you. Stop buying series tickets. You hardly ever feel like going.

GEMINI

THE TWINS
MAY 21–JUNE 21

You are dangerously overcommitted. No wonder you're anxious so much of the time. Stop multi-tasking. Either watch the news or read the crawl. Mercury is your ruling planet, so it's a good idea to avoid fish and get most of your protein from poultry.

CANCER

THE CRAB
JUNE 22–JULY 22

Like your crustacean namesake, you are hard on the outside and tender and vulnerable on the inside, which makes you the center of attention at 12-Step meetings. You like getting into bed right after dinner, where no one can hurt you. A typical cancer, you tend to underutilize your living room.

LEO

THE LION
JULY 23–AUGUST 22

At last you are beginning to mellow. Lower testosterone levels give your loved ones some badly needed relief. With your ruling planet the sun and your element fire, you should wear total block, even in Seattle. Precancerous growths can be removed by a dermatologist, but they leave funny-looking white marks.

VIRGO

THE VIRGIN
AUGUST 23–SEPTEMBER 22

Years of therapy finally kick in. Your high standards still infuriate your friends, but now it's their problem. Yours is lower back pain. It's time to consider a cruise for your next vacation so you won't have to drive or carry luggage. Don't give up on your dream. If anyone can figure out how to fax a pizza, you can.

LIBRA

THE SCALES
SEPTEMBER 23–OCTOBER 23

Feelings of anxiety should subside as soon as you decide whether to buy yet another iPod. By the way, it's not your imagination. The doctor who performed your sigmoidoscopy *was* your paper boy. Loosen up—consider getting a tattoo.

SCORPIO

THE SCORPION
OCTOBER 24–NOVEMBER 21

Your element is water, your planet is Pluto, and your reading glasses are in your jacket pocket. Relax! Dementia's not your thing. Kidney stones are. You will pass them. As long as the lines on your thighs and belly fade by morning, your jeans aren't too tight. It's your skin that's loose.

SAGITTARIUS

THE ARCHER
NOVEMBER 22–DECEMBER 21

You are charming, optimistic, easygoing, and affectionate and have a great sense of humor now that your serotonin levels have been chemically elevated. You are inordinately curious about and proud of everything that comes out of your body. Don't be afraid to ask the waiter to repeat the specials.

CAPRICORN

THE GOAT
DECEMBER 22–JANUARY 19

Stable, mature, and sane from birth, you were born for middle age. You have never had an inner child, a mid-life crisis, or a red car. You are the first in your age group to start commenting on how sloppily dressed and terribly rude young people have become. Winter is getting on your nerves.

AQUARIUS

THE WATER BEARER
JANUARY 20–FEBRUARY 18

Your friends love you for your high spirits, uninhibited ways, and witty voice mails. Try to remember that your sign is water, not asphalt, so unless you're into knee surgery, switch to an elliptical cross-trainer and start swimming laps.

PISCES

THE FISH
FEBRUARY 19–MARCH 20

With water as your element and Neptune as your ruling planet, you are sensitive, dreamy, and hard to reach. Turn up the volume on your ring tone. Stop waiting for the dog to die before you travel. Put him in a kennel. This is the year you begin to think of decaf cappuccino as dessert.

Living Will

of

_____
(PRINT FULL NAME)

_____
(HOME ADDRESS)

_____
(NAME OF LOCAL HOSPITAL)

If the time comes when I am incapacitated to the point that I can no longer actively take part in decisions for my own life and am unable to direct my physician as to my medical care, I wish this document to stand as a testament of my wishes. Should it be determined that I am in an irreversible, persistent vegetative state, plant me.

_____   _____
                                (DATE)

_____
(SIGNATURE)

                           _____
                                (DATE)

WITNESS: _____

                           _____
                                (DATE)

WITNESS: _____

OFFICIAL SEAL